CATCHING UP WITH HISTORY

Books by Matt Simpson

POETRY

Letters to Berlin (Driftwood Publications, 1971)
A Skye Sequence (Driftwood Publications, 1972)
Watercolour from an Approved School (Toulouse Press, 1975)
Uneasy Vespers (Windows, 1977)
Making Arrangements (Bloodaxe Books, 1982)
See You on the Christmas Tree (Windows, 1984)
Dead Baiting (Four Eyes Press, 1989)
An Elegy for the Galosherman: New & Selected Poems
    (Bloodaxe Books, 1990)
To Tasmania with Mrs Meredith (Headland, 1994)
Catching Up with History (Bloodaxe Books, 1995)

FOR CHILDREN

The Pigs' Thermal Underwear (Headland, 1992)
Matt, Wes, and Pete (Macmillan, 1995)

CATCHING UP
WITH HISTORY

Matt Simpson

BLOODAXE BOOKS

ISBN: 1 85224 324 4

First published 1995 by
Bloodaxe Books Ltd,
P.O. Box 1SN,
Newcastle upon Tyne NE99 1SN.

Bloodaxe Books Ltd acknowledges
the financial assistance of Northern Arts.

Cover printing by J. Thomson Colour Printers Ltd, Glasgow.

Printed in Great Britain by
Cromwell Press Ltd, Broughton Gifford, Melksham, Wiltshire.

for John Lucas

'…if you don't read…many a book in summer, ay, and as a friend, drop into poetry too, it shan't be my fault. Now, what'll you read on?'

'Thank you, sir,' returned Wegg, as if there were nothing new in his reading at all. 'I generally do it on gin and water.'

'Keeps the organ moist, does it, Wegg?' asked Mr Boffin, with innocent eagerness.

'N-no, sir,' replied Wegg coolly, 'I should hardly describe it so, sir. I should say, mellers it. Mellers it, is the word I should employ, Mr Boffin.'

DICKENS: *Our Mutual Friend*

Acknowledgements

Acknowledgements are due to the editors of the following publications in which some of these poems first appeared: *Bête Noire, Blue Cage, Critical Survey, Elected Friends* (Enitharmon Press, 1991), *Fat Chance, Give Me Shelter* (Bodley Head, 1991), *Iron, Ladder to the Next Floor* (University of Salzburg Press, 1993) *London Magazine, London Review of Books, Meanjin* (Australia), *Poetry Book Society Anthology 2* (PBS/Hutchinson, 1991), *Poetry Durham, Poetry Review, Poetry Wales, Smoke, Stand, Staple, Stride* and *Verse.*

Earlier versions of 'His Long-Haired One Has a Quiet Word', and 'Ancestors' appeared in *See You on the Christmas Tree* (Merseyside Poetry Minibooks: Windows, 1984).

Contents

Catching Up with History

I could have crossed over (Hope Street was quiet);. I could
have caught up (few were about – a drunk or two,
some dilatory students hugging books); could have said
something. But memory stalled, refused me names. I let it go,

walked on in a fret, a fancy of pictures in long rooms
of painted saints in agonies at fullest stretch,
the gates of heaven about, orgasmicly, to burst on them,
pictures speaking less of Now than of a Just Beyond,
out of reach but guaranteed.

                            Then I remembered
Harry Someone! a man in shabby dungarees, crisp beard,
who rolled his own, nifty with politics and jokes.
Youth Club. Five odd years ago.

                              I whistled Mozart
up Mount Pleasant only to see him suddenly
heading at me, a haggard overcoat and scarf
against the wind. 'Harry? It's Harry, isn't it?' I said.

Harry who looked through me, who didn't want to see
or speak, at whom I shoved my hand and name. Harry who stared
as from another side, through fences and barbed wire,
whose hand I touched. Harry who said 'Life's been
a bitch. Just watch your health. Goodbye.' And went.

Ancestors

I

Press-ganged drunks who woke
in Bully Roberts' hold
or one-eyed Captain Crow's,
who, at slack water when winds veer
and gulls go quiet, looked up
and saw the windmilled heights
of Liverpool wave them away;
slaving men who heard at dusk
all Africa dance, pig-tailed bucks
who ransacked Calabar, clambered out
of Black-crammed holds sweat-drenched
and felt the breeze clamp shirts
ice-cold against them, wind set fair
for Kingston, sugar, rum,
dragging with them wakes of shark.

II

One in particular – and not for merit
(walking upright is a trick of decks)
and not for vices (petty and forgivable,
common enough in him) – he's singled here
for knowing goodness once and meeting it
as such. When booze unselfed him to
a gentler man, he spoke of love with love,
enough to give to failure heart and grace
to bear the sky, the sea, and told
of Kitty Wilkinson, how she put love to work
till something of the city had been blessed.

Blessings go unread, unlooked-for now.
But this is still decipherable:

Indefatigable and Self-denying
the support of the Orphan
the Fearless and Unwearied
Nurse of the sick: the Orginator
of Baths and Wash-houses for
the Poor.

Blackening words. And there's
a stained-glass window if you look for it
where sunlight plays with colours like a child
of Kitty's face among the saints.

If there's a Heaven, then Kitty Wilkinson's
among the meek turning a squeaky mangle
like a barrel organ there.

Kitty Wilkinson: 'During the 1832 cholera epidemic,
without personal or public resources, she prepared food
for the hungry, nursed the sick, cared for unwanted children
and the aged, made her tenement-home available to all, and
used her boiler for the fever-tainted clothing of neighbours;
she once worked for 23 hours continuously at her mangle;
in one week she washed over 170 dozen articles all infected
with cholera. From such selflessness sprang the decision of
the Town Council, in 1842-46, to provide the first public
washhouse in the world.'

PETER HOWELL WILLIAMS: *Liverpolitana*

Anglican Cathedral, Liverpool

'Like God's own Head'

Christ our merchant prince, old money-bags
in frockcoat, toffee-nosed, and well-to-do,

gracious with parks, rhododendron-planter,
best-dressed in sandstone quarried at Woolton,

Sabbath-face reader of lessons from ledgers,
your apotheosis grimed as they built you; before

it was done you'd already turned headstone,
become a skullhead crowned and spiked – blood

like money running out. Once it was
money for old rope. Now it's tears, old sweat:

no joke anymore, blood from stone.

Gifts of Language

I *Carp Fishing*

'Solid!' he gasps and
'Can't you bleedin' help!'

Net to hand and waders on,
I lunge through weed
to budge it, if I can,
his twenty-pounder burrowed in;
lurch through sargassos
where his hypodermic line
jabs in through tangling stems,
where an unexploded bomb
is jammed, and scoop about
till I can raise it, take the strain,
relax both rod-and-line and him
who gives me this:

'God, me heart is pumpin' piss!'

II *With Tom and Maud in the Granny Flat*

Tickled by her old Catholic-Liverpool comebacks,
those Things-She-Keeps-Coming-Out-With,
their doggedness and mental double-jointedness
that's Irish as the Blarney Stone is long,
he wonderfully provides for her, fusses her pillows,
fetches things on trays. She has us all in tucks.

Even today a neighbour's death is glossed
'If the Good God spares me meself'll soon be dead.'

III *In Case*

Fear of losing
clutters the house with junk,
oddest things with absolute
talismanic authority. No use
protesting or dissuading.
She has her reasons.

Reminds me of a shifty shipwright

in a dockside warehouse
gushing odour of oranges,

muttering as he fingered
a three-foot length of oily rope,

'This'll come in handy, even if
I never find a use for it.'

IV *Tactile*

A green bus bumping down the dock road home, top deck
chock-a-block with caps and smoke and burliness. A donkey man
scours a window with his sleeve to make a great smudged O
as we fidget to a halt, watches as a blonde climbs in,
pelmet of skirt yanked tight against her rump,
earrings clanging as we rev and jerk. He leans across:

'Wouldn't mind slippin' 'er a goldfish, mate!'

V *Imagists*

'Coughing like an old tugboat,' they called,
and 'One more clean shirt for you!'

As the old tug tightened hawsers into iron,
'Solid muscle them!' he said.

What Isaac Chapel Told the Wordsworths

Told him thank you sir
and your good missus. Heard
her say Beloved. Twice.
That word in her, as in
the Song of Songs, was sweet.

Master said she was
his sister. My mistake. A kitchen fire
I quickly said is wholesome to
a man been trudging three
long days from Liverpool.

Then spoke at their request
of my adventures. Brutish thing
this being press-ganged sir,
hauled over bruising cobblestones,
a sack of coal no less,

flung under hatches, sobering up
in swaying creaking darks
impatient, greedy to be off
beyond the slimy estuary. Twice
I swam ashore at night and once

was cast away, trekked a month
with North American Indians.
That Maxwell sir, now there's a brute,
captain on the Guinea run,
a flint-hard, scowling slaving-man.

One man killed, and then a tiny lad
lodged in with pigs that bit at him,
half-dead, another set there in the sun
at watch until he croaked. That Rogue
I'm here in England to appear against!

Two hours' warmth and nourishment,
I headed west for Whitehaven.
Missus says she had another brother
looks like me by name of John. Master
calls himself a poet. Very like.

Shore Leave

... most seamen lead, if one may so express it, a sedentary
life. Their minds are of the stay-at-home order; and their
home is always with them — the ship.

CONRAD: Heart of Darkness

Indeterminate weeks of grey,
ennui that comes with letting time,
a coat too long upon its hook,
lose shape: dolphin unmiraculous,
one-after-the-other waves, the sky
a same old stared-at thing
graffiti-sprayed with stars.

Yet when gulls come scavenging in,
and there's the sniff of land again,
despite myself, I muster up
a coy belief in goodness for the time
I step once more on stone;
feel the way she edges in,
fenders groaning lustfully...

Worst when we berth where I was born
because I know the city will
have changed again, become
more derelict. Maybe
I'm better anchored in my bunk,
shelf of books to hand. For all
they say of home, it's where you're used
to being more than any other place.

A rigger hurls a whiplash rope
that, missing, falls, then stings
the glutinous water of the dock;
taxis, women, pulsing, wait. I head
for shops where students have
off-loaded books they can't afford
to keep, books to slither,
totter when the waves
get high and my small space
rocks about in space as if
something's set on chastening.

The indeterminate weeks at sea
become determined hours ashore: I do
the same things over every time,
clatter gangways, follow streets
to their conclusions on the clock.

Three Stones in Childwall Parish Churchyard

*

Stranger, passing by,
Pause awhile and think,
That I am in Eternity
And you are on the brink.

No let-up; even from the grave
the sales pitch bangs away.

From this ground-hogging slab,
Gothic black,

lichen-green,
some Beloved's finger wags,

frock-coated culture spouts
its parables. Beneath this stone

a hell-bent shaft is whizzing down
to extremest kinds of forfeiture.

*

Over here, would you believe,
a poet? A once-beloved of Tennyson.
Who threw his laurel in the ring
when Bridges got the job. Knighted too.

WILLIAM WATSON, POET.

So estranged from this
City of festering streets by Misery trod
his widow sneaked his coffin in by night
down the suburban avenues.

*

This place also delivers a knock-out irony,
the ending-up too early here of a friend of mine,

a kidder on a brutal scale
cutting the ground from under you...

now floored and shiny-stiff in polished jet,
gilt letters putting him among the Named,

all dressed up for spoil-sport Sundays,
with nowhere to go, no way for him to wriggle out.

His Long-Haired One Has a Quiet Word

Him over there, him with the rum 'n' peps,
old Tragedy Kecks himself... likes to think
he's just stepped down the gangway off
a Blue Star boat, bag slung across
his shoulder like a rolled-up tent...

back from around the world and letting on
he's come-day-go-day and quids-in,
when really it's a policy matured I scrimped
for all these years. Face on him? Face all right!
Back-end of a train smash. All codology...
him in his come-in-the-jigger suit
from Paddy's Market, knocking back as if
he's only got tomorrow left.

      Lived with him
long enough to know he's putty all inside,
and, God, he's old enough to understand...
slobbering over yesterdays, shinning up
ropes to spy out landfall, staggering quays
of foreign ports, in some flash bar,
some Lulu snaffling all his pay.

      But that
was donkey's years. And what's the rest?
No bungalows in Wales for me, roses round
the door. A maisonette until the cows...
And her above us, her five kids,
and telly blasting all the livelong...

       just look,
he's in another world, in Callao, Rio, Hobart,
Trincomalee with all his salty mates.

Prufrock Scoused

Less juss shin off me an yooze
seein as ow its as soddin borin as
someone avin der appendicks out.
Lets juss bugger off down ere
where thee ardlee is no one
where the moanin minnies toss n turn
in the doss ouses or Yatsiz Wine Loge
where thee spew der rings up
an piss on the floor down streets
that go fuckin on-n-on like some beady-eyed
bastid big-ears luckin fer a barney
an tryin t catch yer out not knowin sumpin.
But dont gerrin a tizzy doin yer ed in
juss fuck off down there anyroad.

Ders diss posh do wid lah-di-dah judies
janglin about ow thee once-t knew John Lenin.

Foggy out. Luck arrit tru d winder
like sum jigger rabbit, sum jowler prowlers
smudgin the glass or lappin up yuck
outer d gutter scratchin the bin bags
slinkin off den jumpin up orl ov a suddin
curlin roun the ouses before gerrin its ed down.

Yeah OK it can do dat
when it wants to if it likes an no messin.
Yooze yerself cud purron yer come-in-the-jigger suit
an go out an marmalise someone or not. Depends.
Tons of bleedin time – hours – fer the both ov uz
t juss dick around or not, even...
dreamin yer life away or buckin yer ideas up
before tuckin in t yer bacon butties.

Orl dem Lady Mucks is still at it!
Wen ar thee gunna give over eh?

Arent I right tho? Yiv gorr-ages
t cack yerself if thats what yer fancy
y cud even scarper if y wants.
Ah God eh, the bastids-ll call uz Baldy Ed
(bald as a bleedin melling thee-ll say!)
Me wid me duck suit on, tie an everythink,
orl decked up like the Cunt of Monty Cristo
(bet thee call me friggin Neck Ends!)
Just oo the fuck am I den?
I'm no redskin with arl the answers thats f sure.
I cud juss snuck out off ome
an wotch Blind Date on the telly.

An yer not gettin one over on me neether!
I been there ar kid!
Orl them brew ups I put down me
an everyone clammin up wen I walks in.
So juss tell uz oo the fuck am I, Wack?

Its the way thee orl gorp at yiz
as if yiv juss come over, callin yer
a wally behind yer backs.
OK, so I'm a dosey-arsed bastid
so wot? Its ardlee werth
undoin yer flies for, never mind
takin off yer kecks.

Dem posh judies, I know der likes
fur coat an no nickers the one arf ov dim.
(Cant elp fancy the one or two tho!)
Ten t one dat ones Oh-dee-Klone over der
is puttin me off me sarnies.
Mind you some bobby-dazzlers too!
But oo am I tell me?
Any case worra y gunna come out wiv?

Sumpin like diss? Excuse me luv
burr'I seen orl the owld geezers on ther tod
smokin ther Woodies. Reckin dats enuff do yer?

Shud juss pack it orl in! Dats about
the size ov it. Eer yare tart, wanna fotie?

22

The avvo, the evenin avin a birrova kip
jerked off if ther jammy or praps
shagged out, or simplee angin the latch, eer
nex terruz on the arth rug.
After arl the swiggin an the bevvyin
I don't think I'd get me end away now anyroad
eevin if I wantid. Like someones sliced yer ed off
an brung it in on a tea tray like yer John the Papist.
Makes no odds, no skin off my nose.
I'm norreevin in the make-specks wen it cums
t judies. Anycase the chucker-out looks
like eez gunna yocker on uz on the way out.
Gods onest trute, I woz creemin meself.

Ooze t say itd do any good after anyow
scoffin yer cornflakes, sippin Typhoo
orl dem orniments on the winder ledge
the pair ov uz yakkety yackin over ow good
a shag it woz or not, then gabbin away
like Father Bunloaf about capital ell friggin Life
as if Lazzerus cum back from the Udder Side
t say worrits like. So bleedin wot? Speshly if
some ot kecks tart turns roun an sez
call tharra dick!

Big ook eh? Know worr-I mean like?
After orl the arsin about…ard to purrit
inter werds… but like seein yerself
on ome videos pullin soft arsed faces.
Wot wud be the use if sum
snotty nosed little Tilly Mint went an told yer
y werent on afterorl?

That thingee by Shakespeer, Amlit is it?
Well dats not me, I'm no Rhubarb Vaselino
I'm more y can-lad, doin odd jobs
sweepin up an tha, sumtimes even
suckin up t the blockerman, now an aggen
a titchy bit lah dee dah, burr OK reelly
sumtimes wen I'm not coddin meself
a birrova twat.

Not gettin no yunger neether. Worrabowt me
all toney, kecks up t the knees at New Brighton?

Do I go the Swenys fer a short back-n-sides?
Gerra curry from the takeaway? Juss you see me
in me dago kecks cockin an ear t the seagulls janglin

thee bloody ignor me them lot!

I seen them messin about roun Gladstn Dock
an dive bombin the Royl Iris.

Reckin I need me bumps feelin
gettin orl gooey over the thort of a feel up
in the sand dunes at Formby.

'Eh yooze mate d wanna nuther bevvy?'

Couple
(for Anne Stevenson)

Gave up the sea
to live alone

with her;

sat
and watched

snooker players cue
order out of randomness,

jockeys whip
luck to meanings –

colours and numbers,
a hierarchy

of constellations,
heaven

in a dull kitchen.

*

She
lived alone with him

and watched
him watching,

eyes

rancorous, hating
his heaven/haven,

his company
of hosts, his

pot-shots and horseflesh,
his liquid-rattling breath.

The Common Touch

on the 50th Anniversary of the Battle of the Atlantic, and for S.P.

The "exile" of the poet is symbolical and always represents, paradoxically, a "homecoming".

I

On a day like this
of rain and rattling helicopters,
flags slap-slapping
like smacked behinds,

on a grey day like this
obstinate as Tory doctrine, a time
of soggy handshakes and glum smiles,
when the stuff of war's brought out

of mothballs and buffed up,
and lachrymose old men
march past with rows of dashing gongs
to validate

Monarchy and Country yet again,
on days like this
I wish that I was neighbouring you
in Flinders, Oz,

under a democratic sun
and what you've called authentic life.

II

Your unsettled and unsettling visit here
was more subversive than you'd hoped:

I took you to the Albert Dock (where that
phlegmatic pageant's underway now as I write)

where our conversation drifted on an open sea,
on currents we thought might bring us to

landfalls lush in poetry; dawdling over coffee
by the Maritime Museum, watching kids with clipboards

converting wonder into usefulness, 'That takes me back,' you
smiled, meaning the pretty schoolteacher. So

we talked lost moments and lost loves (a trade
in guilts for sounding friendship out),

until the place's fakery and smarm became
too much. 'What was this once?' you asked.

Once? Creak of gantries winching bales,
bawl of blockermen doling out day's work,

those unlucky shambling off to pitch-and-toss
somewhere against a jigger wall:

folk-memory spooks! Lashed to the quay in front of us
a replica – reminding us how puny things

once dared great deeds – Drake's *Golden Hind*.
Round-the-world is easier now; suave telly voices gloat

Australia's a day away;
you sit at ease through everything.

So imagining you, head above clouds, chasing home
(your home from home), poems tinkered over Everest,

is easy too: all you do is sit it out,
walk the tarmac, find a cab.

III
The Atlantic Battle rattles on. Today's
wind is whipping up grey History
to service po-faced ceremony,
rain's rat-tatting on Drake's drum:
Queen's reviewing her warriors, stiff old men

with re-awakened loyalties. A day like this
I wish I were out there with you
walking the shore in search of scallop, clam,
and periwinkle – shells of the harmless sort;
perhaps with dark-voiced Tsaloumas,

poet of the heart's incorrigibilities,
richer by exile, full of Yeats's old-man gaiety,
we could sleep out overnight
close to the pier in that van of his,
then in Australian sunlight chase the shark.

Greetings from Tasmania
(for Tim Thorne)

Think of clustering apples. The garden tree
of clambering fruits that almost drag it down;
a warehouse overwhelmed with smell of them,
apples winched from holds, stashed crate
on crate; the scent of landfall after weeks
at sea. The apple isle!

                       My poems are away
sightseeing. Package tour. Thumping
iambic feet down-under now. With genuinely
interested faces, everything to declare.

They want to see the back streets too –
especially those! – to sniff out corners where
my old man after weeks at sea wound up. Some
fifty years ago. The Maggie Mays of Hobart then.

Mailing back the weather, wishes we were there,
looking for family likenesses.

Millet's *The Gleaners*

Watch out for the bloke astride the horse –
the blocker-man – keeping measured distances

between himself and us, between us and
the fixed horizon, hedges ending fields;

puissant and upright for now – though vertical's
a better word – with such an arrogance between his legs

there only needs a twitch of rein, a squeeze of thigh
to curb its titillating twitchiness

or spring its energies, velocities on us.
Keep backs to him and keep your distances,

fidget your fingers in the stubble. That's
the language he allows:

consonants, vowels of breaking backs,
sibilance of grain.

On My Mother's Side

Across the double-glazing, the full moon
nudges a lookalike, its own spook satellite,
in and out of watery cloud.

A quartet's refined accents – *andante cantabile* –
are exercising heart strings
when, gurgling suddenly, the phone...

She's trying numbers, Simpsons in the book.
'Is that the Matt Simpson that's at
the Liverpool University?' Dear Cousin Marge.

There's just enough love between us now
for announcing funerals, opening graves.
She tells me now her father's slung his hook;

an old heart, straining to lift a clod, a spade,
has juddered to its halt. And snipes 'You sound
posher than the last time you and me...'

(another year, another grave); reprimands 'That's not
our Mattie!' I need to joke 'Diss better den?'
to help her feel at home, put her in some kind

of right, so's we can be all-those-years-ago
hardfaced again. It's my mother's brother, John,
twenty years outbreathing her. His Seventy-Five

is throwing shadows now that I'm my mother's age.
Much of my life his man's-world excluded me:
the pubs, the bevvying, docks, grabs, slings,

his docker's hook slashing into cotton bales...
that khaki photograph, sergeant's cheeriness,
cap skew-whiff across his brow as if

appalling war were his best joke. Years collapse
in ten minutes' trite apologies, regrets,
voices wriggling in and out of graves.

'We thought you ought to know,' they say.

Easy Chair

God knows how long,
my little finger wormed
the cigarette-burn's
tight black hole,
how long, once he had gone,
I stroked the leatherette
as if it were a chestnut filly's haunch:

same armchair
where he, my aunt's new 'chap',
double-breasted, quiffed,
last Sunday sat
fidgeting a cup,

who just that day before
(grandad circled the details with his glass)
had netted the ball for Liverpool!

The parrot had been curfewed,
velvet curtain over the cage,
not a word upon its beak –
a strangled whistle now and then,
a scratch of claw.
                    But it was Sunday,
there was celery and fairy cakes,
and, famous for an afternoon,
everyone in the family knew the score.

What happened to it?
Doris's inside-right,
with his First Division suavity,
engaging Errol Flynn moustache,
she never married?

Words, words, no one wants to hear,
velvet curtain over things.

Here's me, too late by donkey's years,
telling it over, God knows why,

twiddling that little finger still.

Books My Grandfather Gave Me

I dared their bedroom once. That
oppressive, different century.

Grown-up bed, white lace, a scrubbed
deal table, jug-and-basin's bright
polar chastities, brass-looped chest
of sea-swag bullied back through oceans
out of lands God privileged with sun,
palms shadowing crescents of white sand.

Their history looked innocent.
Perhaps looked innocent to them?
Genteel disembarkations from blue-
green seas. Imperial benevolences.

Places meant to smile forever
in books of patiently tooled engravings.
Delicate shadings so fine you feel
you could blow them away like ash.

Coincidence

We end up here
in a shabby chapel;

expecting it to rain
or threaten to;

in sorry huddles
shaking cousins' hands;

uncertain if to stand
or sit or kneel,

or how much voice to give
to words we would have liked

to leave behind in school;
totting up what's left

of years, of wondering;
and holding on to wonder

as something we attach
ourselves to meaning by:

the aunt that says
'It's twenty years

to the very day
your father died.'

Write Off

These childhood streets have nothing left to say.
Mouths puckered tight on secrets – remorse
or pleasures more prosaic than
ones I've wanted to regret. No trick of shade
or sunlight livening a wall, a rotted sill
is like to tell me different. I'm out
of transformations now. This must be the last attempt
before the place has grown impossibly small
on me – a bloated Gulliver straddling roofs.

Enough's already swilled down gutters – all those
grotesqueries: bonfires, and tough
soft-hearted women, swaggering men,
clanging bin-lid warfare on bombed sites
as fierce, as much obsessed with what is just,
as heroes on the battered plains of Greece.

This front garden was never big enough to bury in,
its crazy paving crazed so long it's driven off
what ghosts I wish might once have haunted it.

Nights in the Gardens of Spain

Splashed arpeggios, tinkled pianissimos,

sul ponticello strings and distant horns. Water

honoured in fountains, water's sanity on hot

half-conscious nights that thrum *¡Soy er fuego*

en que te abrasas!

Recalling nights in Barcelona,

a city dreaming itself. Bodega floorshows – Goyescas:

hunchbacks, beanpoles, negro dwarves. Cackles, smoke,

spilled beer. *¡Soy er mar en que naufragas!*

Or a languid dream of saunterers, dawdlers on

the Ramblas. *No sé qué siento, ni sé qué me pasa*

except to gesture a fair exchange: nakedness

for nakedness in a green room. Blotched breasts,

nipples she wants to hide, and my virginity.

An oyster squelch. Dripping seaweed. Sudden. Strange.

Illicit in Grasmere

Darkness of hills. And behind hills
further darknesses. Vividly hushed.
A conspiracy of grass and trees.
Palpable as where a mole sniffs,
as underwater-eyes-closed swimming is.
And warm. A summer night tucked in.

A climb to a field, barbed wire that snicks
trousers at the groin. A fumble
to extricate and then on grass to penetrate
to even deeper darknesses. With cows
approaching, munching, munching.

Too Much

That's good, that's enough.
TESS GALLAGHER

There are times – she knows them too (they are banal enough) –
I'm stumped for what to do or say: as when again tonight
I dithered at the gate in slippers thin enough to feel the damp;
her in white anorak chivvying kids to their back seats
after they'd been too much hugging me for an afternoon of goonery;
when I know she too – too simply – wants holding and a kiss;
her mouth girlish, combative; mine sensible, refusing, knowing what
is best. Gratefully/ungratefully watching tail-lights pull away.

Reader I Never Married Her

a riot of a week in which
a pissed-off friend
bashed his skull into oblivion
gritting on
the easiest/hardest answer to...

free-falling from roof tiles
joyfully as if he'd cracked
it finally...

it's whisky talking and the sky tonight
continuing hysterical: I'm full
of windy sentiment – that stuff
about remembered love, that
jabbing purity of longing for...

why, wherever you are, don't you
miraculously turn up
to grin some bloody sense
back into me?...

should be speaking volumes
not these blind free-falling words:
need your eyes, your hand...

Rochester calling...

Gaelic Lament

I wonder if
you remember enough
to want to hear
this piece in ways
I sometimes do;

whether, for fear
(from wear and tear)
of losing track,
like me you went
from vinyl to cassette,

upgraded to CD,
to digital remastering?
Remember that first time –
twenty years ago?
you played it through

those two-way speakers
in your flat, even then,
the second the stylus touched,
the music was
tangy with farewells,

a piper on a bluff
keening to waves
of trans-Atlantic ghosts
that the clearances
and famines carried off,

lament that defined
a harrowing silence
of the sea. Even then
I knew that we
would graduate

from silences
to silence,
silence which
this music
ruthlessly defines for me.

Out of the Blue

(for Vivien)

The relish of coincidence. You ringing me
to tell you've jagged a muscle in your back:

both prostrate, me the couch and you the hard
straightness of the floor. I'm ahead.

My pain has had a fortnight to mature. I speak
with some authority, grumbling what it's like,

what to do, what not. Being masterful.
Easy on the telephone. Your pain springs

from grandchild clamourings too:
'Lift me, lift me, lift me up!' Dangerous

toddling things. And so ('Don't make
me laugh! it hurts!') we joke

that there are nicer ways of ricking backs.
Life trundles out its old regrets again,

wishes things were sexier. Well,
let's relish our coincidence, though we know

its signifying smile's a fraud; keep soft spots
for what-might-have-been, its glow.

Helvellyn

You say we should go back there,
where we, hand catching hand, left
imprints, hobnails scuffing rock,
scree scuttering a thousand feet;

and see the place as history, as more
than somewhere wind and cloud
make wordless bargains; where we climbed
the teetering vertebrae of Striding Edge

that kept dropping back into their own space;
watched the graphite tarn contract,
pucker, wince below; piled ourselves in stones
upon the summit cairn; then hobbled down

the rainy western side to Wythburn chapel
and the road – Helvellyn, an obdurate past
separating and coupling us,
whalebacked above us and behind.

FOUR FOR MONIKA:

Clearing Out

is something I threaten, dream of more these days,
clambering out and tramping shell-shocked back
past glumly marshalled others moving up the line,

gone forever-fishing, tranced by ripples, leaving behind
this over-lived-in house which we've re-roofed,
repainted, double-glazed, which never quite shrugs off

its thought of others gone before, their hedges,
built-in wardrobes, square-cut lawns that always keep
me dutiful. A few years' mortgage left to run, a couple more

to pension, and still our old dynamic yanks me back:
my if-only's, your yes-but's alive enough
to neuter choice. Clearing out today's rhetorical again,

shambolic shuffling off, before plumbers arrive
to unbolt, rip out, replace the old boiler, so we become
economical with heat. Chucking out from this

one corner, I'm at least creating gangway, room,
ruthless in the way that you are holding on to things.
And it makes you edgy, this not honouring

your kind of remembering. When you quote time and place
you know of things exact to wind or wound me with;
not *when* but *where* is where I'm good: streets, roads,

bookshops, pubs. You won't relinquish hold. Your
just-in-case with screwtops, coffee jars, cartons,
envelopes, plastic bags, and me, is you surviving war

you hardly think is over. This outhouse clutter's
bin-bagged now. But I can't be sure you won't
go rooting cat-like, rummaging in the dark, clawing back

mildewed curtains, sandals without buckles,
carpet off-cuts coughing dust, handbags without handles,
coddling the past in some other precious hidey-hole.

Reported Missing

I'd go if I could. I'd take a thousand pounds
like our friend Jan who just tramped off
to Tibet to find out more about death. I'd buy
a sensible anorak, back-pack, and go,
leave tomorrow, except you need to keep me here;

not just because I'd cock up your birthday,
the grandchildren coming, the cake, but because
you daren't trust yourself enough to think
that I'd come back. And yet I'd like to go
on some forlorn adventure soon... let's say

to trace (there is the slimmest chance he's still
alive) the father who fifty years ago marched out
on you, who, under orders, (weren't they all?)
trudged into Russia through unimaginable snows.
His grey old photograph (when people thought

photography was theft and always looked afraid)
declares a bookish horn-rimmed man
whose unpreparedness is plain. I like to think
he dragged his rifle wearily into that blizzarding
East. **Reported Missing**'s where I start.

I'd bring him back if it meant healing you
of half a life's distrust. Maybe he did slink off
into a wood, and over mountains, made it back
in time to see the rubble of Berlin; perhaps
like my father, home from sea, among the bricks

of our bombed street, he shrugged and thought
he'd come too late. I can't pretend it isn't
hazardous. Telly daily pounds buildings
into rockeries, borders shift with the tide,
men with rifles dodge round pockmarked walls.

You can count on crossfire, mortar shells, mines,
the old historical certainties. I think it would
be worth it. But then that's me talking. Tomorrow's
your birthday, the need to brave it out again.

Tending

After years of promises, I managed
to get round to it this time, as one might
with a second honeymoon, an eternity ring,
or re-papering a room: I daubed both front
and back with showy annuals, cheap, ground-
hugging plants to hide the soil.

Petunias did best, keeping a vulgar riot up
for months, flashy fairground sassiness beyond
first frost and rot of leaves. The roses had
been manicured, blasé far too long, an outré
aristocracy with keep-your-distance thorns.

Tiddly-pom and the thrill of the circus, love.

Enough grounds here for doing it again.

That Old Feeling

Elgar, Famous Grouse, and a summer night
with nothing much in mind. Except to flirt
with clichés. O.K. Clichés are
only truth with some immediacy
rubbed off. Memory's loitering with intent
of something sensuous; love wanting to feel
itself again. Recapture/rapture if I were
in rhyming Ella or Sinatra mood.

I'm hoping for a particular night
of thirty years ago. Simon loping round to that
old murky Cambridge flat of ours and you
beautiful in pregnancy. He was expecting too:
First Novel any day – go-ahead and anxious,
dead ringer for Eliot at Harvard in 1906.

I've doubts of his remembering this. We didn't
keep in touch. You remembered: the talk,
the jokes, and how he said
you hardly looked...
                    That night you woke me up
we had no coppers for the phone,
we packed some things and walked a mile
to Mill Road Hospital. The stars were beautiful.

* * *

The Nine Lives of Sukie

There have to be more than two,
the two I can account for,
unless we say your first
was too spectacular to merely count

as one: the time that you,
mechanic's rag, were found
beneath the bonnet of a car
someone had driven thirty miles.

And number two? The day
you risked a dash across the street:
weekend in Intensive Care,
broken jaw, the loss

of feeling in one leg. Must
have been others that
we never knew about – squawking nights
behind hedges, ear-tatterings,

forfeit-lives. Can't believe
that seven came together here,
in this corner of a room
so precipitously. Too quiet, subtle,

too catlike. As if you were
keeping an appointment. As ordinary
as that. There's profound
absence though. Hardly a corner of

the house you didn't appropriate:
wardrobes where pullovers pile,
each window sill, the patch beside
the bathroom door that your unfailing bum

sussed out as where hot water pipes
ran underneath; and, when I'm at
the windows looking out, those spots
you knew the sun preferred.

Imagining the Worst

A bullet with my name on it!

This morning clacking shears
rattled a sick-bear's bandaged-head
of wasps. The secret life of hedges!
I had stumbled on warlords muttering.

A million bullets in a war to kill a man!

Dive-bombed, strafed,
I fell through clouds of pollen,
smacked between the eyes.

Poplar Root

The bugger's come a hundred yards,
sniffing drains, the garden pond,

spade-shaped leaves the giveaway,
bonsai, heaving up between

flags; and here without a by-your-leave
snapping three-inch concrete into chunks

like a kid with fudge, greedy
wanting dark and light, both up

and down, and ever on. It's going to take
some rooting out, levering of slabs,

hard slicings into stubborn clay:
the garden a toppling graveyard,

exhumation taking place. This is
a Dracula-stake-and-mallet job – I mean

a shovel's amputating edge, creosote
to tar hacked bones... after which

replace, repoint, build up again, just hope.

Windy

A fidgeting wind
is in off Ireland,
in from the black
Atlantic beyond,

itching fingers wanting to work
the gritty scalps of Wales,
in a night that's sure to be
scatty with sleeplessness again.

Already across
the gull-huddled estuary,
down the curves
of a sick Mersey,

you can feel solemnity,
as if a dropped
subject has been taken up again
and you must resign

your anxious grip on dream, on hope
risen above themselves again.
The neighbourhood is battened down
in dull moods of content,

lives made neat and justified
by purchase, television trance,
or by sleep's nothingness.
The wind is in the hedges

scouring out truths they needn't face –
here, right here –
even when the weather breaks.

Good Samaritan

(for Maurice Rutherford)

At proximus meus quis est?

Expect denial; understand
his truculence, this man resenting kindliness:

there's something to admire
in the surly syllables that order me to fetch
his ladders in, ladders he's just fallen from.

Not enough to unhook him from his shears,
limp him to his door: there's
this terrible flimsiness leans on me,
one leg buckled, crumpled under us.

I'm a bit afraid, asking if
there's anything else for me to do, like put
the kettle on, get someone for him to the phone.

He's saying nothing, hates
the cliché of it all, another face-to-face
with brute-force sense. He wants me gone.

Just can't leave it there; knocking at
five neighbours' doors, find only one that knows
even his name: 'Keeps to himself,' they shrug.

'But someone ought to know and I live miles from here.'

A nervy missis calls her husband out
who doesn't want to, but he nods,
shambles across the road, is gone
behind the old man's half-cut hedge,

its clippings blowing down the road.

A Requiem Mass
(for Eileen Hughes-Crean, 1948-1994)

Introitus

A road right-angled
to the river;
estuarial smells,
bladderwrack,
decaying kelp,
oily mud and tar;

rows of crumbling villas,
behind which skulk
sandbanks, seagulls hunch
against cold winds,
with turned-up collars,
ticking minutes off
to yet another turn of tide;

and between the houses,
west towards Ireland,
a glimpse of horizon,
that old Beyond-Which of
this city's history;

and further illusion
of fixity: the church
I'm heading for,
a Gothic upwardness
to God-on-High,
a Come-In from
those earnest people
at the gate.

Here they'll try
to soften into yearnings
that timor mortis which
your death unloosed.

Kyrie

Sense of being late,
something crepuscular,
sniff of incense, sharp
as mould, taste of rust
between the teeth. Late
in the culture, late
in history. Dusty books,
mawkish icons, strained
deliberateness.

Never *too* late –
they all tell you that.
It's a knowledge:
how music becomes memory
altered in repetition:

this adagio of Haydn's
they are performing here
is a sort of epitaph,
a wreath in sounds
placed on a coffin
by people I know nothing of,

music that from now will have
a stale funereal whiff to it,
a woman's troubled face in it,
a wistfulness,
a melancholy vagueness;

                    I'm awed
at all the people that you knew,
the crowded pews, the hats,
whole classes in school uniform;
I fumble pages for the words
they know, who also know that this
is music that you specially chose
the week before you died, the week
you whispered down the phone to me
'God bless!'

Graduale

They say you chose your coffin too.

Offertorium

The game of likenesses. Who is he like,
this priest?... priest who now intones
that you're in Heaven, how in the Glorious
Fullness we'll meet up again.

Who's he like? Pudgy cheeks and Van Dyke beard
...myself ten years ago.

Means what he says. Kindly too. And yet
the humanity of it doesn't fit
the dwarfing vastness of this place
with all its crystal echoings.

Sanctus

Round the black, cumbersome coffin,
a family says farewells it does not choose
to see as gone-forever goodbyes.

How brave they are! What is it fortifies
that reason won't undo? How can I put
an Allelujah into this?

Agnus Dei

I remember you
in my tutorial room,
after just one week
desperate to give up.

Wrong choice, wrong choice
you said and wrung your hands.

Then driving out
the College car park,

cigarette-hand on
the wheel, convinced
that I'd bamboozled you.

Those seminars on *Hamlet*
where you were
ambitious to know everything.

Now your degree is honorary:
and in anticipation,
there are photographs
of you in gown and mortar board,

all in a garden green,
among your smiling family,
a consorting springtime sun.

Only your face shows
the illness that attends...

And now the quartet's playing Borodin.

Communio

Goodbye, Eileen.
I'm heading back to College now
through roads that I grew up along:
streets named after poets,
roads after Earls; the church
I trebled, tenor'd in; schools
that tuned me to the sounds of words,
and cowed me with their authority.

Goodbye, Eileen: your priest declared
that Life Goes On. And so it does.

The music's serious love,
its loving seriousness, which you
are folded into now, spoke deeper than
ever could his words or these –
though with the same intent – of mine.

Three Men in a Boat on a Blank Day

I

'Remember Tabley? Must be
ten years. The day we ...' Yes, it's time
to break the ice. The day we made

a serious winter effort after pike,
deep into a frozen-hearted county, hard
against the weather's lore.

Formal arrangements had been made –
you phone to hear the agent's voice
distantly professional –

to pick up oars just after dawn
the gamekeeper will put out for you
beside his musty shed.

It's said that Eisenhower slipped out
of battledress to sit among
the big-house silver there, was roundly told

its summer fame for red-eyed tench
bubbling in the lily pads
and susurrating reeds.

We had tested it, those fish
with honeyed flanks,
and found it so. But this

was winter, there were ploughed-up fields
to drag our tackle, bait and oars across,
furrows hard as chunks of glass.

II

He hadn't said the mere was silver-thick
with ice, one patch of open water
at its top end like a black half-moon.

Three men in a boat kicking a jagged
loop-the-looping line through ice
for two hard hours. And not one

pike spun out that day from the black
water we arrived at; no barbs
jagging at jaws; no green-

and-yellow tigered sides hauled up
on board; no black eyes glowering;
and nothing said of it until today.

III

Three men in a boat – a constable,
a lecturer, a town-hall clerk.
Two have kept in touch at Christmas with a card,

linked only by the other's death
and the memory of a silver-plated mere
one empty winter day.

Beginner's Luck
(for John Sweetnam)

*

You wanted to learn freshwater craft.
I took you to a spot where I had found
rainbow trout would hit a bait
like uppercutting fists.
The only tackle you had brought
a stiff glass-fibre beachcaster
used on North Wales shingles where
tides came hissing in, where you tried out
the temper of the bass.

'Got one!' you shouted jerking back
your titan rod. An 8oz spangling fish
went hurtling back behind us fifty yards
and crashed among grey boulders
without benefit of priest.

*

Then pike-fishing. I took you to the Dee,
a spot I knew was good for spinning in.
It rained, it sleeted; wind drove in
its knives. And there was nothing doing. Who
would be the first to ask
what's showing on the Box? To want to know
what this morning's post had brought?
'Let's go, eh?' I chattered. And we did.

That night you phoned. On your way home,
you'd dropped by your local lake.
Guess what? A nineteen-and-a-quarter
pounder pike had buckled your best spinner
first cast in.

After that you searched
your area for likely spots. One day you quiz
a gaffer about fishing in a lake
beside a factory and behind meshed wire.

I want to believe you were not kidding
when you told me his reply: 'Pike? Ooh ah!
There was a pike in there would crawl
out up the bank and bark at passers-by.
They had to shoot it in the end!'

November on the Streets

Tell the truth Dad pissed me off and Mam
could never cope. I'm on my own
and watching out for winter now. Cold wet fart
roused me this morning in a travel agent's door.

I've learnt a binbag mac keeps out the rain
and polystyrene warms your soles;
Guardian and *Times* lag best; you keep *The Sun*
to twist a jamrag for your bum.

Remember remember the fifth of November –
coat off a guy, or kecks; and two left shoes
knocked off from outside Timpson's are
better than no shoes at all.

Empty paint cans burn and, after, you can boil
one for a brew. Back of Tesco's
for dumped unlabelled tins – mostly cat and dog –
but now and then you hit on ravioli, mince.

Down the cemetery, diggers' cabin's good,
stove still warm, enough tobacco shreds
around the floor to make a roll. It's out
the wind, the way.

Cold morning piss-smells and white tiles
where you wash, where you never take
off coats. Look out for Number One's the game.
There's always someone needier.

An Hour or So in Heptonstall

(for George Szirtes)

We walked through obligatory rain over the too-
many dead, across the words and numbers meant
to mean them. Doves clattered in a hollow tower.

The gone-before were mumbling under stones, words
just faintly carrying: *Love, remember me,*
I only sleep. The one grave we had come for was

a caved-in chest, collapsed cage of ribs.
For all the talk of *golden lotus* and *fierce flames,*
the roses there were lingerers, pathetic clingers-on:

better that gothic fantasy of week-old wreaths
in brittle brown and black about the newest grave,
their look of things abandoned or let-be.

It's not the dead who speak, of course,
it is ourselves are pleading love, remembrance,
insisting what we mean. This gravestone's words

take no one in for long. Yet like the roses
we can't let go: the soil's possessiveness and dark
are where the growing's done.

Helen Thomas Visits Ivor Gurney in the Asylum

Here's a map a dead man tramped;
and here too on the bed a clutch
of flowers he might have picked
for her to bring. No vases though.
In here a vase is death. The flowers
are something brought in on the wind.

Fingers ramble lanes, trudge hills,
linger by churches, halt thirstily at inns,
stray into meadows where Edward hears
rooks' black songs, where Ivor promises
a swan-like end, fading in music.

It's too much. They falter, fumble at
a dead-and-buried pastoral. Their map
is too like trenches now – lines
wandering everywhere and nowhere
through shell-shocked Gloucestershire.

A Note on Implement 48
(in memory of W.S. Graham)

> *It is only when the tenant is gone*
> *The shell speaks of the sea.*
>
> 'Implement 48'

Got me at it now
asking who I'm talking to
out there in the ocean-going winter dark.

Is it really fourteen years?
Where's that far-back Pamela
with her resolution to give smoking up?

What's the odds she ever did? – that night
she was quite resolved
to do it for her daughter's sake,

night of difficult dangerous ice,
petrified streets, life
at hazard, limbs unsafe

as if already we were rotten drunk.
Who am I telling? My friends
Maurice, John might like to listen in. Perhaps.

It's a blinking cursor eggs me on: I've said
'already' so we know
there's more to this. That hard night

imagine Pamela and me
slithering streets in quest
of extra whisky for a poet we had left

propped against a mantelpiece
in Mount Street. She was the one
who watched his drip-feed shrink.

Fifty years'
bad boozing on his breath
already smelling of his death

(now rhyme has caught us unawares).
Which selves did he protect
and which allow for speaking in?

What words, between healths,
could we have confab in
before darkness/bottle swallowed up?

Fourteen years ago it was
and seven more was all he got
before they put him down (his word)

the manhole. Let's disclose
something that came later from him
April '81 – a wind of gannets and

Scotch whisky blowing up from Cornwall –
'I'm making new poems. Easy,' he said.
'I just make them up out of my head'...

(there's incidental rhyme again!) Make them up?
Something of that. And yet it seems
someone's or something's coming through

from the Other Side. On screen,
contemptuous of full stops,
the cursor throbs imperatives.

Crabs

Sureness and accuracy:
the fisherman knows his job.

I watch the cleaver drop:
each muddy crab is cracked in two,

a concern for symmetries,
a summary justice.

It is perhaps the crabs' own crass
attempts at pattern he despises,

the stupidity of overdoing it:
deformity in that great claw, the way

it makes them scissor sideways,
scuffling through mud.

He'll show them symmetry! What's
more telling than two halves?

Scrapes them with the cleaver off
the plank into a crate. They fall,

a clatter of knitting needles.
Hoses down as if they'd never been.